W9-AFF-086

Spies in the Civil War

Untold History of the Civil War

CHELSEA HOUSE PUBLISHERS

Untold History of the Civil War

Spies in the Civil War

Albert A. Nofi

CHELSEA HOUSE PUBLISHERS
Philadelphia

The author is grateful to Derek Schiaronne for reading and commenting on the manuscript. Also to Mary S. Nofi for putting up with yet another project.

Produced by Combined Publishing
P.O. Box 307, Conshohocken, Pennsylvania 19428
1-800-418-6065
E-mail: combined@combinedpublishing.com
Web: www.combinedpublishing.com

CHELSEA HOUSE PUBLISHERS

Editor in Chief: Stephen Reginald
Managing Editor: James D. Gallagher
Production Manager: Pamela Loos
Art Director: Sara Davis
Director of Photography: Judy L. Hasday
Senior Production Editor: LeeAnne Gelletly
Assistant Editor: Anne Hill

Front Cover Photo: Courtesy of Tradition Studios © Keith Rocco

The Chelsea House World Wide Web site address is
http://www.chelseahouse.com

First Printing

1 3 5 7 9 8 6 4 2

Library of Congress Cataloging-in-Publication Data applied for:
ISBN 0-7910-5427-6

Contents

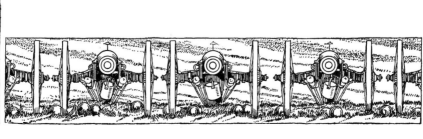

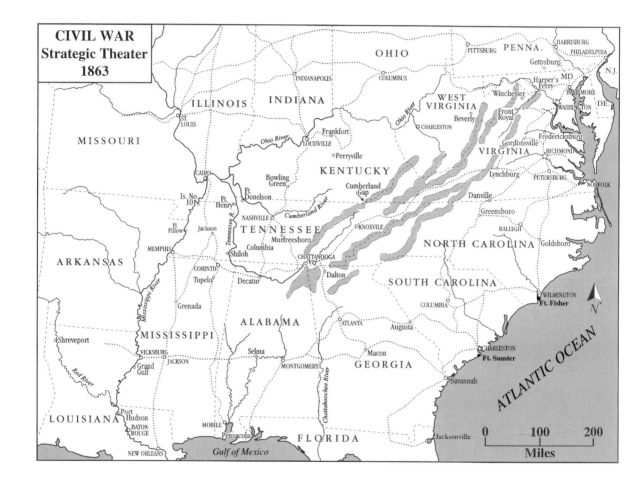

CIVIL WAR
Strategic Theater
1863

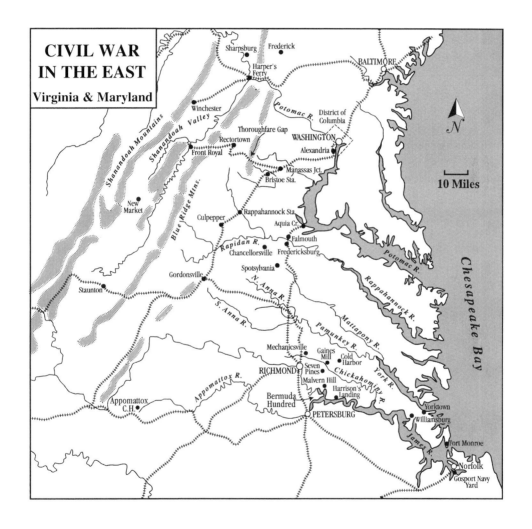

**CIVIL WAR
IN THE EAST**

Virginia & Maryland

N

10 Miles

Sharpsburg
Frederick
Harper's Ferry
BALTIMORE

Winchester
Potomac R.
District of Columbia

Shanandoah Mountains
Shanandoah Valley
Thoroughfare Gap
Rectortown
WASHINGTON
Alexandria

Front Royal
Manassas Jct.
Bristoe Sta.

New Market
Blue Ridge Mtns.
Culpepper
Rappahannock Sta.
Aquia Cr.

Rapidan R.
Falmouth
Chancellorsville
Fredericksburg

Gordonsville
Spotsylvania
Potomac R.

Staunton
N. Anna R.
Rappahannock R.

S. Anna R.
Mattapony R.

Mechanicsville
Pamunkey R.
Gaines Mill
Cold Harbor

RICHMOND
Seven Pines
Chickahominy R.
York R.

Malvern Hill

Harrison's Landing

Appomattox R.
Bermuda Hundred
Yorktown

Appomattox C.H.
PETERSBURG
Williamsburg

James R.
Fort Monroe

Norfolk
Gosport Navy Yard

Chesapeake Bay

Civil War Chronology

1860

November 6 Abraham Lincoln is elected president of the United States.
December 20 South Carolina becomes the first state to secede from the Union.

1861

January-April Mississippi, Florida, Alabama, Georgia, Louisiana, and Texas also secede from the Union.
April 1 Bombardment of Fort Sumter begins the Civil War.
April-May Lincoln calls for volunteers to fight the Southern rebellion, causing a second wave of secession with Virginia, Arkansas, Tennessee, and North Carolina all leaving the Union.
May Union naval forces begin blockading the Confederate coast and reoccupying some Southern ports and offshore islands.
July 21 Union forces are defeated at the battle of First Bull Run and withdraw to Washington.

1862

February Previously unknown Union general Ulysses S. Grant captures Confederate garrisons in Tennessee at Fort Henry (February 6) and Fort Donelson (February 16).
March 7-8 Confederates and their Cherokee allies are defeated at Pea Ridge, Arkansas.
March 8-9 Naval battle at Hampton Roads, Virginia, involving the USS *Monitor* and the CSS *Virginia* (formerly the USS *Merrimac*) begins the era of the armored fighting ship.
April-July The Union army marches on Richmond after an amphibious landing. Confederate forces block Northern advance in a series of battles. Robert E. Lee is placed in command of the main Confederate army in Virginia.
April 6-7 Grant defeats the Southern army at Shiloh Church, Tennessee, after a costly two-day battle.
April 27 New Orleans is captured by Union naval forces under Admiral David Farragut.
May 31 The battle of Seven Pines (also called Fair Oaks) is fought and the Union lines are held.
August 29-30 Lee wins substantial victory over the Army of the Potomac at the battle of Second Bull Run near Manassas, Virginia.
September 17 Union General George B. McClellan repulses Lee's first invasion of the North at Antietam Creek near Sharpsburg, Maryland, in the bloodiest single day of the war.
November 13 Grant begins operations against the key Confederate fortress at Vicksburg, Mississippi.
December 13 Union forces suffer heavy losses storming Confederate positions at Fredericksburg, Virginia.

1863

January 1 President Lincoln issues the Emancipation Proclamation, freeing the slaves in the Southern states.

May 1-6	Lee wins an impressive victory at Chancellorsville, but key Southern commander Thomas J. "Stonewall" Jackson dies of wounds, an irreplaceable loss for the Army of Northern Virginia.
June	The city of Vicksburg and the town of Port Hudson are held under siege by the Union army. They surrender on July 4.
July 1-3	Lee's second invasion of the North is decisively defeated at Gettysburg, Pennsylvania.
July 16	Union forces led by the black 54th Massachusetts Infantry attempt to regain control of Fort Sumter by attacking the Fort Wagner outpost.
September 19-20	Confederate victory at Chickamauga, Georgia, gives some hope to the South after disasters at Gettysburg and Vicksburg.

1864

February 17	A new Confederate submarine, the *Hunley,* attacks and sinks the USS *Housatonic* in the waters off Charleston.
March 9	General Grant is made supreme Union commander. He decides to campaign in the East with the Army of the Potomac while General William T. Sherman carries out a destructive march across the South from the Mississippi to the Atlantic coast.
May-June	In a series of costly battles (Wilderness, Spotsylvania, and Cold Harbor), Grant gradually encircles Lee's troops in the town of Petersburg, Richmond's railway link to the rest of the South.
June 19	The siege of Petersburg begins, lasting for nearly a year until the end of the war.
August 27	General Sherman captures Atlanta and begins the "March to the Sea," a campaign of destruction across Georgia and South Carolina.
November 8	Abraham Lincoln wins reelection, ending hope of the South getting a negotiated settlement.
November 30	Confederate forces are defeated at Franklin, Tennessee, losing five generals. Nashville is soon captured (December 15-16).

1865

April 2	Major Petersburg fortifications fall to the Union, making further resistance by Richmond impossible.
April 3-8	Lee withdraws his army from Richmond and attempts to reach Confederate forces still holding out in North Carolina. Union armies under Grant and Sheridan gradually encircle him.
April 9	Lee surrenders to Grant at Appomattox, Virginia, effectively ending the war.
April 14	Abraham Lincoln is assassinated by John Wilkes Booth, a Southern sympathizer.

Union Army
Army of the Potomac
Army of the James
Army of the Cumberland

Confederate Army
Army of Northern Virginia
Army of Tennessee

Secret Service officers at Army of the Potomac headquarters in Virginia, February 1864.

I

The Spying Game

"*This way, Gentlemen.*" *Confederate president Jefferson Davis led his secretary of war and General Robert E. Lee into his private office in Richmond, Virginia. As the visitors took seats, Davis rang for a servant. Then he also sat down. They began to talk.*

In a few minutes there was a knock at the door.

"Come in," said Davis.

A young black woman entered. She wore a bandana on her hair and an apron covered her simple dress. "Yes, Mr. Davis?"

"Tea for three, Mary."

"Yes, Mr. Davis," replied the young woman.

A few minutes later the young woman reentered the room. Deep in conversation, the three men took no notice of her. On a tray she carried a pot of tea, cups, saucers, spoons, a little pitcher of milk, a bowl of sugar, a dish with several slices of lemon, and a little platter with an assortment of cookies. She quietly arranged these on a side table. Then she turned to leave.

Davis spoke, "Thank you, Mary."

"Yes, Mr. Davis," she replied as she left the room.

About two hours later the three men left the room. Within a few minutes the young woman reentered the office. Working quickly, she stacked the tea fixings on a tray. She wiped off the side table. Several documents were carelessly scattered on the desk. She arranged these into a neat pile. As she did, she looked over each. Most she put down quickly. A few she read carefully. Then she swept the floor. In the wastepaper basket, she found several crumpled pieces of paper. She carefully opened each, to examine their contents. Then she returned them to the trash. A few minutes later she left the room.

Later that evening, her day's work done, the young woman left the Confederate White House. She walked through the night the few short blocks to the home of Elizabeth Van Lew. There the two women wrote down what Mary had heard and read and Elizabeth encoded the information. Later that night it was hidden in a loaf of bread. A courier carried this through the Confederate lines to the Union forces outside of Richmond.

Mary Elizabeth Bowser was no ordinary slave. A highly educated, free woman, she was also one of the most effective spies in American history.

Some of the most ancient records from Sumer, Egypt, China, and other early civilizations mention spies. They even appear in the Bible. Spies have had an important influence on many historical events. But espionage—the use of spies—has never been something people spoke very openly about. It was not considered "honest" or "fair." Until the 19th century most countries had no systems for gathering valuable political and military information called "intelligence." When major political problems or wars occurred, they had to rush to set up an intelligence service. This was particularly true of the United States.

During the American Revolution George Washington had proven to be a very good spy master. But for most of its history the United States did not have an intelligence service. Sometimes the president or another government official would make special arrangements to gather information. Often he would quietly contact someone who knew something about the situation. Or a friend would be asked to take a "vacation" or "business trip" to see what he could find out. Sometimes army or navy officers were placed on "detached service." They would travel somewhere in disguise to collect information. Even in wartime things weren't much better organized. During a war certain government officials and generals were given money for "secret service" operations. But they had no training in how to organize these operations. They had to pick people they thought might make good agents. Some agents they selected proved good at their jobs. Many were not. The people selected were usually untrained. They often lacked the imagination necessary to be a good spy. Or they were not good at disguising themselves for long periods. They might not understand what information was important and what was not. Nevertheless, this was the only "intelligence" service that the United States had in 1860.

In November 1860 Abraham Lincoln was elected president. Many Southern states began to secede from the Union. Officials of these states began sending people on missions to collect information. Federal officials began to do the same. Soon the spy war was underway months before the first shots were fired in the Civil War in the spring of 1861.

This depiction of the life of a spy in the Civil War sketched by Thomas Nast appeared in Harper's Weekly's *October 24, 1863, issue.*

II

Spy Masters, North and South

*T*he Union's espionage effort got off to a poor start. For most of the first year of the war no one was in charge of collecting information. The State Department had some agents, the War Department had some too. Many individual generals had spies. Even some state governors had agents.

Allan Pinkerton became the Union's first spy master. He was a private detective before the war broke out. One of his clients was the Illinois Central Rail Road. Pinkerton had served as Lincoln's bodyguard when he went to Washington to be sworn in as president in March of 1861. A few months later George B. McClellan, the railroad's president, became one of the most important generals in the Union army. He made Pinkerton head of army intelligence. Pinkerton was good at catching spies and uncovering plots. After all, that work was essentially detective work. But he was not as good as a spy master.

Pinkerton's methods of choosing agents were odd. He sometimes hired agents based on phrenology. This

Allan Pinkerton, head of intelligence operations for the Union, (left) stands with President Abraham Lincoln (center) and General John A. McClernand on the fields of Antietam.

James A. Garfield, considered to be the best spy master for the Union army. He later became the 20th president of the United States.

is a superstition like astrology. It assumes that character, intelligence, and skills can be determined by examining the bumps on a person's head! Obviously this was not a good way to select intelligence agents. Worse, even his experienced detectives were not trained to gather *military* information. They often had trouble estimating the number of troops in a military formation, often greatly overestimating the number of Confederate troops. Pinkerton reported that the Confederates had between 180,000 and 200,000 men. But many Confederate regiments were only at about half-strength as most had lost men due to sickness, battle, leaves, or transfers, so the Confederates actually had only about 80,000 men. This was a very serious mistake because McClellan was a very cautious general. Once he actually received a copy of Confederate General Robert E. Lee's orders, but did not act on the information. Pinkerton's estimates caused McClellan to be even more cautious and led him to miss several chances to win battles. When Lincoln fired McClellan in the fall of 1862, Pinkerton went too. After Pinkerton there was no one person placed in overall charge of intelligence operations.

Major General William S. Rosecrans who, as leader of the Union Army of the Cumberland, had James Garfield as his spy master.

Political intelligence was collected by agents of the secretary of war, Edwin M. Stanton. More purely military information was the responsibility of the generals in the field. Each general assigned an officer to direct intelligence operations. Some of these officers did a good job. Some didn't. Gradually those who weren't very good were replaced by men who were. One of the best was James A. Garfield.

Garfield was a lawyer in Ohio when the war began. He joined the army in August 1861 and by January 1863 had fought in many battles. Garfield was promoted to brigadier general at 31 years of age. He became chief of staff for the Army of the Cumberland in Tennessee. As chief of staff he managed the operations of the army for its commander. The army had no intelligence chief. Each division commander had his

Pauline Cushman, one of the spies for the Army of the Cumberland, provided invaluable information to General Rosecrans. She was eventually captured, tried, and sentenced to hang. But she managed to escape and reach the Union army where she was greatly admired for her bravery.

own scouts and spies, and these agents gathered a lot of information. But this information wasn't analyzed very well, nor was it always passed on to those who might be able to use it. Garfield began having all the information passed to him. He read the reports and evaluated the information. Then he prepared summaries for his commander, Major General William S. Rosecrans. Garfield soon became an expert at information management. He became the best military spy master in the entire war, on either side. For example, in June of 1863 he estimated the strength of the Confederate Army of Tennessee at 41,680 men, only about 9 percent too low. That same month his estimate that the Confederate commander in Tennessee had sent 12,000 men to Mississippi was only 6 percent too high. These were very accurate estimates. But his greatest achievement was to collect the information that permitted his commander to carry out the Tullahoma Operation.

In June 1863 there were 65,000 Union troop in Tennessee as opposed to 45,000 Confederates. Garfield knew where all the Confederate troops were. Garfield and Rosecrans used their superior information to trick the Confederates. They pretended to attack the western side of the front where the Confederates were strongest. But meanwhile they began moving strong forces around the Confederates to the east. These forces moved very rapidly. They soon threatened to get into the Confederate rear and so the Confederates had to retreat. By July 4, 1863, nine days after the Army of the Cumberland had begun to move, the Confederates had retreated 100 miles. Although there had been some fighting, there had not been a serious battle; Union losses were less than 600 men killed or injured. Garfield had provided the information necessary to force the Confederates from their position with a minimum of fighting. By the end of the war Garfield was a major general. He entered politics and in 1880 was elected the 20th president of the United States.

Like the Union's espionage effort, the Confederacy's had no head. The president, the secretary of war, the secretary of the navy, and individual generals all had their own agents, as did some governors. But often the information they gathered was not distributed prop-

Colonel G. Moxley Sorrell supervised Confederate General Longstreet's spies and scouts.

erly, and sometimes valuable information was available but not used. There were some capable Confederate spy masters though. One of the best was Colonel G. Moxley Sorrel. A 23-year-old bank clerk in 1861, he was a private in the Georgia state militia. He served as a volunteer aide to Brigadier General James Longstreet at the battle of First Bull Run, and his efficiency impressed the general. Eventually he became Longstreet's chief of staff. Some historians believe Sorrel was the best chief of staff in the Confederate army. One of his jobs was to supervise Longstreet's spies and scouts, one of whom was the mysterious "Harrison," among the best spies in the war. Sorrel proved very good at this work. But in October of 1864 he was promoted to brigadier general and given a combat command. Though he proved an excellent combat soldier, the Confederacy lost the services of one of its best spy masters. After the war Sorrel was a merchant and shipper. His book, *Recollections of a Confederate Staff Officer,* is one of the few reliable memoirs about espionage in the Civil War. He died in 1901.

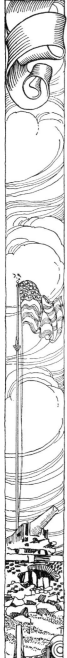

III

Master Spies of the Union

*A*s we've said, at the start of the Civil War the Union had no intelligence service. The first agents were army and navy officers who volunteered to undertake risky missions for the president or General Winfield Scott. During the tense weeks before the outbreak of the war Navy Lieutenant John L. Worden traveled in disguise through the South to gather information about Union forces holding Fort Pickens at Pensacola in Florida. Captured on his return trip, he spent months in a Confederate prison. After he was exchanged, he commanded the famous ironclad *Monitor*. During this same period Union Captain Peter Haggerty disguised himself as an organ grinder—complete with monkey—and roamed the streets of Baltimore during the first days of the war in April 1861 in order to spy on pro-Southern activities in the city.

Military officers serving as spies were soon joined by amateur spies. Union sympathizers living in the South often sent information to people in the North by vari-

Two soldiers are pictured getting information from a black man along the road. African Americans were important sources of information to the Union army.

ous secret means. Not all of the amateurs were actually useful. For the Union the most valuable amateur spies were the black people of the South. African Americans knew that a Union victory would mean the end of slavery. Whenever Union forces were in an area, they would attract fugitive slaves. These people were usually willing to supply information. Of course they were not familiar with military things. So at times the information was confusing or inaccurate. Still, careful questioning and analysis usually led to useful information. These people also knew the local geography. Fugitive slaves often served as guides for better-trained agents. And some black people, both slave and

free, served as spies themselves. Slaves are "invisible" in a slave society; the masters are so used to their presence that they are not usually noticed.

Many African Americans performed just one mission and never undertook another. For example, Mary Touveste was a free black woman from Norfolk, Virginia. She made her living as a hired servant. In late 1861 the Confederates began converting a wooden, steam warship into an ironclad. The Union navy was very concerned about this vessel. Touveste got a job at the home of an engineer who was working on the ship, the famous *Merrimack*. He kept important plans and documents at his home and Touveste was able to

Mary Touveste helped the Union navy get information about the new Confederate ironclad, the rebuilt Merrimack, *here shown in its famous battle with the* Monitor.

examine these and even copy some of them. Then, in February of 1862, a few weeks before the vessel was completed, she disappeared. By means of the Underground Railroad Touveste made her way to Washington. There she gave the information to the secretary of the navy. This helped the navy to prepare for the great battle between the ironclads *Monitor* and *Merrimack*, which took place early in March. Mary Touveste had only undertaken one spy mission. But it was an important one.

There were many other notable Union spies and below are stories of just a few:

"Crazy Bet" Van Lew and Her Spy Ring. The most successful espionage network of the Civil War was run by Elizabeth Van Lew. Born in New York in 1818, by the outbreak of the Civil War she was rich, unmarried, and very plain looking. She had grown up in Richmond, Virginia, but was an abolitionist, opposed to slavery. When her father died, Van Lew and her mother freed the family's nine slaves.

When the war broke out Van Lew decided to serve the Union. At first she helped Union soldiers who were prisoners-of-war in Richmond. With her mother she would bring them food and clothing. This made most Southerners think of her as a little odd. Van Lew decided to become odder. She began to dress carelessly and to express open opposition to the Confederacy. People were amused by her peculiarities and she seemed harmless. They nicknamed her "Crazy Bet." All of this provided excellent cover for her secret activities. The soldier-prisoners often provided Van Lew with useful information about the war and she smuggled this information to Union forces. Van Lew had a farm outside of the city. She would send people on errands to the farm to bring back milk, eggs, and other products—they would also carry concealed

messages. From the farm, other agents would carry the messages to still other agents, and eventually the information would reach Union commanders.

Van Lew also helped soldiers escape from Confederate prisons. Once she helped more than 100 men escape by means of a tunnel. She hid many escaped prisoners in a secret room in her house—the same house in which she rented a room to the commander of one of the Confederate prisons!

Eventually Van Lew's spy ring included dozens of people, men and women, black and white, slave and free. Samuel Ruth, the supervisor of the Richmond, Fredericksburg, and Potomac Rail Road, was one of her agents. His job was to move supplies and troops for the Confederate armies in Virginia. Ruth was an expert at "making haste slowly." He seemed to work very hard to get supplies to the front. But he was actu-

Elizabeth Van Lew ran the most successful spy network of the Civil War from this house in Richmond.

ally working to delay shipments as much as possible. Ruth sometimes could turn a four-hour railroad trip into a 40 hour one. Since the soldiers often moved by rail, he was able to pass on information about Confederate plans.

Another of Van Lew's agents was Martin M. Lipscomb. He was a merchant who handled supplies for the Confederate army. This meant he had to know something about Confederate plans. Lipscomb pretended to be such a loyal Confederate that he was almost elected mayor of Richmond. And then there was Philip Cashmeyer. Cashmeyer was probably the main reason neither Van Lew nor any of her agents were ever caught. He was a detective who worked for Brigadier General John Henry Winder, the Confederacy's chief spy catcher—he was also a Union spy. But the most important of Van Lew's agents was Mary Elizabeth Bowser.

Bowser was younger than Van Lew and a former slave. When they were children someone had given Bowser to Van Lew as a playmate and the two girls grew up together, becoming close friends. As soon as she could, Van Lew freed Bowser and sent her to live in the North where Bowser received an education and became a teacher. When Van Lew decided to go into the spy business she asked her friend to return to the South and help.

Bowser was an enormous asset to Van Lew's work. She pretended to be a slave. In Southern society a slave was almost invisible. In this way Bowser could pass through Confederate lines while carrying messages to Union commanders. But Bowser was even more valuable as a spy working in the Confederate White House. Unfortunately the details of the story will never be completely known. After the Civil War Van Lew asked to have all records of her work and burned them. So we only have a general idea of what happened.

In mid-1864 Confederate president Jefferson Davis and his wife Varina decided to hire a maid. Van Lew arranged for Bowser to get the job. As a slave, Bowser had virtually free run of the Davis's quarters, including the president's office. She had many duties—dusting, polishing the silver, cleaning the windows, looking after the Davis children and their pet squirrels. As Bowser went about her duties, she was able to read— even copy—some of the most important documents in the Confederacy. Sometimes she served lunch or dinner to Davis and his top political and military advisors. She kept her ears open as she worked.

Each night, Bowser returned to Van Lew's house. Van Lew would write the information down using a special cipher, sometimes using milk, which makes an invisible ink until the paper is heated. Van Lew would then pass the information on to Union commanders outside the city. She had several ways of doing this. Sometimes she gave the message to a baker who came to the house each day to get eggs and milk. He would bake the message in a loaf of bread. The bread could then be smuggled through the Confederate lines. At other times messages were hidden inside eggshells. Sometimes messages were concealed in the sole of a boot, and would "walk" to the Union army. Van Lew's messengers were very careful. None of them were ever caught. They were so efficient, it is said that they often delivered flowers from her garden to Union General Ulysses S. Grant as his army lay camped outside Richmond late in the war.

Not until early 1865 did the Confederates begin to wonder about possible "leaks" from their White House. Van Lew and Bowser were probably tipped off by Philip Cashmeyer. Taking $1,500 from the Davis residence, Bowser fled Richmond. This made her seem to be just an ordinary fugitive slave, rather than an escaping spy. For a time Van Lew was under suspicion of espionage. But her eccentric ways and outspoken support for the Union made most people think she was merely a crazy old spinster.

Neither Van Lew nor Bowser did well after the war. When Van Lew's wartime activities became known her neighbors avoided her. Since she had spent virtually all her fortune in the Union cause, she sank slowly into poverty. In 1869 the new president, Ulysses Grant, made her postmistress of Richmond. But she lost this job when Grant left office in 1877. After that she was supported by donations from many of the soldiers she had helped escape from prison. In her old age she was a very lonely woman. She died in 1900. Bowser's fate is unknown. Upon her escape from Richmond she fled to the North and soon afterward she vanished without a trace.

Timothy Webster, Masterspy. Timothy Webster was born in England. He came to the United States as a young man and became a policeman in New York City. Webster was a very good policeman. He came to the attention of Allan Pinkerton, head of the only private detective agency in the country. Pinkerton hired Webster and as one of Pinkerton's agents, he worked on a number of cases for the Illinois Central Railroad. Early in 1861 Lincoln was preparing to go to Washington to be sworn in as president. Rumors began to circulate that he was going to be assassinated by pro-Southern agents. Lincoln's friends convinced him to rely on Pinkerton for security.

Pinkerton sent Webster to investigate the rumors and he soon uncovered some conspirators. He alerted Pinkerton, who changed Lincoln's route, getting him safely to Washington. Soon Pinkerton was made the

Timothy Webster became a double agent working for the Union cause.

chief of what would today be called "Army Intelligence." He asked Webster to be one of his agents. On one of his first missions in the spring of 1861, Webster went to Memphis, Tennessee, where he pretended to be a Northern supporter of the Confederacy and made friends with Confederate soldiers. They let him visit their camps and fortifications. From Memphis he went by train into Mississippi, then across Tennessee again and on into Kentucky. By the time he returned to Union territory in Cincinnati, Webster had a lot to report. He knew the strength and location of the Confederate forces in the region and was also familiar with the design of many of their fortifications and the condition of the railroads in the area.

Confederate secretary of war Judah P. Benjamin hired Timothy Webster to spy for the South not knowing he was already a spy for the North.

That summer Webster was asked to spy on Confederate-sympathizers in Maryland. He managed to join the "Knights of Liberty." The Knights claimed to have 10,000 men ready to attack Washington from the north when the Confederate army in Virginia attacked from the south. Webster was able to reveal the plot to Pinkerton. The whole organization—much less than the bragged about 10,000 men—was arrested. To protect his cover Webster was among those members arrested, but he soon "escaped." This convinced most Confederate sympathizers that he was one of them.

During the autumn of 1861 Webster began a series of missions to Richmond. On one of these trips he had to cross the Potomac River by boat. With him in the boat were two women and three children, going to join their families in the Confederacy. A terrible storm came up that swamped the boat. Webster was able to rescue the two women and two of the children. This made him a hero in the Confederacy. He was introduced to the Confederate secretary of war, Judah P. Benjamin. Benjamin offered to make Webster a Confederate agent and Webster accepted. His mission was to carry secret messages to Confederate agents in Washington. This made him what would today be called a "double agent"—while pretending to work for the Confederacy he was actually working for the Union. With information Webster provided, Pinkerton was able to round up many Confederate agents in Washington, including some in the War Department and other important positions.

While in Richmond in January 1862 Webster came down with rheumatism. He was confined to his bed in a hotel. For weeks he could not communicate with Pinkerton. Pinkerton sent two agents to see if they could find him. The two men, Price Lewis and John Scully, found Webster, but they were not very good agents. They were soon arrested as Union spies and were sentenced to be hanged. To save their skins, they turned Webster in.

Although very ill, Webster was arrested. Tried, he was sentenced to be hanged. Despite pleas from Lincoln and others, Webster was executed on April 29, 1862. Pinkerton said of Webster, "No danger was too great for him." Webster was the first American executed as a spy since Nathan Hale during the Revolutionary War. During the Civil War about two dozen men were eventually executed as spies by the Union, while the Confederacy executed over 60 people, including one woman.

Sarah Emma Edmonds, a.k.a. Franklin Thompson. Franklin Thompson was an expert at disguise. In fact, even Franklin Thompson was a disguise. For Thompson was actually a woman! Sarah Emma Edmonds was born in Canada and moved to the United States before the Civil War. When the war began Edmonds disguised herself as a man, and using the name Franklin Thompson enlisted as a male nurse in the 2nd Michigan Volunteers in the spring of 1861. The regiment was soon sent to join the main Union army in Washington. In the spring of 1862, Edmonds learned that the army was looking for volunteers to serve as spies. She studied everything available about the geography of northern Virginia and the military situation. Then she volunteered. Allan Pinkerton found "Private Thompson" highly qualified, and hired "him" immediately.

On her first mission Edmonds disguised herself as a young black man named "Cuff." She darkened her skin with silver nitrate and wore a wig. For a couple of days she helped build Confederate fortifications and later served as a cook. Then she escaped back to Union lines, bringing valuable information. Even when she was interviewed by General McClellan she concealed the fact that she was really a woman. A short time later she undertook another mission, disguised as a fat, Irish, lady peddler. Edmonds was able to sell some of her goods in a Confederate army camp while gathering information. To escape, she stole a horse, getting away in a hail of bullets, one of which wounded her in the arm.

Over the next year Edmonds—whom everyone still believed was a man—undertook many more missions behind Confederate lines—in northern Virginia, the Shenandoah Valley, and Kentucky. She sometimes disguised herself as "Cuff," at other times as a young white man or an old black woman. In Louisville, Kentucky, she masqueraded as a rich pro-Southern young man, in order to spy on the activities of people secretly supporting the Confederacy. Altogether she undertook 11 spy missions. Between missions, Edmonds continued to work as a male nurse. By the spring of 1863 she was serving as a nurse with Union forces at Vicksburg, Mississippi, when a problem arose—she came down with malaria and had to go to a hospital. But that would mean her true identity would be discovered. So Edmonds deserted from the army. She became a woman again and entered a private hospital. When she recovered, she could no longer return to the army since Franklin Thompson was listed as a deserter. She decided to enlist as a woman nurse and worked for the rest of the war in Washington.

After the Civil War Edmonds wrote two volumes of memoirs, *Unsexed, or the Female Soldier* and *Nurse and Spy in the Union Army.* She married and had three children. In 1884 Congress awarded her a military pension for her services. She died in 1900.

IV

Master Spies of the Confederacy

*E*arly in the Civil War the Confederacy did well in the spy business. Even before the fighting began in April 1861, officials of the Confederate government began sending agents to collect information. Southerners who worked for the Federal government passed a lot of information to the Confederacy. There were even army officers and clerks in the War Department who were secretly working for the South. For a long time there was no effective Union counter-intelligence service to hunt spies. In addition, early in the war the armies were very small, and it was difficult for Union forces to patrol the long frontier with the Confederacy. Agents passed easily from one side to the other.

There were a number of notable Confederate spies. Some of them became famous. Many others we will never know about as their exploits were never told. Often it was the least famous spies who had been the most effective. Here we relate only a few of the many stories known.

Belle Boyd served the Confederacy for many years often flirting with Northern soldiers to obtain information.

"The Rebel Joan of Arc." Belle Boyd was 17 years old when the Civil War began. She lived in Martinsburg, in the Shenandoah Valley of western Virginia. It was a very important region. An army marching north in the valley could easily invade Maryland or Pennsylvania. The valley was also a rich farming region, and during the war it supplied much of the food for the Confederate armies in Virginia.

When the war began Boyd wanted to do her bit for the Confederacy. She decided not to disguise herself as a man and join the army, as some other young women did. Instead she became a spy. Boyd had many interesting adventures. One of the most notable occurred in May of 1862. Confederate Major General Thomas "Stonewall" Jackson was campaigning in the valley against superior Union forces and towards the end of May Union forces began a series of maneuvers intended to trap him.

At the time Boyd was living behind the Union lines and there was a young Union officer living in her house. Although she was not very pretty, she had a pleasant manner and a nice figure, and was daringly pro-Confederate. The officer fell in love with her and they became engaged. Since this officer worked at Union headquarters, she knew that he had access to some important documents. One day Boyd noticed that he had a packet of papers sticking out of his pocket. As they were kissing, she swiped the papers without his noticing. The papers revealed the location of Union forces in the Shenandoah Valley, some 30,000 troops. Disguised as a boy, Boyd rode 15 miles at night through forests and across mountains. She had to dodge Union patrols several times but she got the information to Stonewall Jackson and it helped him win the battle of Front Royal on May 23.

Boyd's main "technique" was to flirt with soldiers, get whatever information she could, and then pass it on. During the war she was arrested several times. The first couple of times she was let off lightly—it wasn't considered proper to imprison or execute women in those days, even if they were spies. Finally, in July 1862 she was locked up in Washington and that December was sent south in a prisoner exchange.

Confederate General Thomas "Stonewall" Jackson was assisted in the Shenandoah Valley by Belle Boyd's information.

The Confederate government sent Boyd to Europe as a courier but her ship was intercepted by a Union vessel and she was captured. Union navy Lieutenant S. Wylde Hardinge promptly fell in love with her, and tried to help her escape. He was arrested and she was deported to Canada. From Canada she went to England. Since she was now pretty famous, Boyd worked to drum up support for the Confederacy. She acted in little plays about her adventures. Meanwhile Lieutenant Hardinge was thrown out of the Union navy. He traveled to England, and married Boyd in August 1864. Boyd convinced him to become a spy for the Confederacy and while she remained in England, he returned to the United States. There he was arrested, thrown in jail, and later died of disease. A widow at 21, Boyd continued to work on the stage. After the Civil War Boyd returned to the United States and supported herself by acting in plays about her adventures. She wrote her memoirs, *Belle Boyd in Camp and Prison.* Unfortunately it is thought that she made up a lot of what she put in her memoirs and so it is hard to tell how good a spy she really was. Belle Boyd died in 1900.

Rose O'Neal Greenhow. "Wild Rose" was born in 1817. By the time the Civil War broke out she was a witty, educated, wealthy, and attractive widow of 43, with a young daughter. Greenhow was a prominent member of Washington society. She often entertained high-ranking government and military officials. Greenhow had been one of President James Buchanan's closest friends and was even a guest once of the Lincolns at the White House. But Greenhow was also an ardent secessionist. The newly formed Confederate States of America soon had agents out recruiting people to serve as spies and Greenhow was recruited by Captain Thomas Jordan. He was a United States army officer who was now working for the

Rose O'Neal Greenhow and her daughter Rose are shown here in Washington, D.C.'s Old Capitol Prison, where she was held as a Confederate spy.

Confederacy. Greenhow became the Confederate spy master in Washington.

Washington was full of Confederate sympathizers and Greenhow quickly put together a large spy ring that began operating even before the fighting began. Greenhow had agents in the War Department, the Navy Department, the Adjutant General's Office, and the Senate Military Affairs Committee. She even recruited agents in the Provost Marshal's Office, which was supposed to catch spies! Her agents included other well-connected, wealthy citizens, ordinary people, and even a dentist.

Greenhow's first big success was probably her most important. By the summer of 1861 large armies were gathering. There were 35,000 Union troops in Washington and 18,000 more at Harper's Ferry, at the northern end of the Shenandoah Valley. The Confederates had only 22,000 men in front of Washington and 10,000 before Harper's Ferry, so Union forces outnumbered the Confederates by nearly two-to-one. To improve the odds, the Confederacy needed to know what the Union plans were. Greenhow went to work. She romanced a senator who served on the Military Affairs Committee and also the secretary of the general in chief of the army. Soon she had information on the Union plans. Greenhow prepared a message for Confederate General Pierre G. T. Beauregard. She gave it to Bettie Duvall, an attractive, rich, young Washington woman. Duvall hid the message in her hair, dressed as a farm woman, and made her way through the Union army's lines in a grocery wagon. Within hours she delivered the message to Beauregard. The Union troops at Washington were to advance on July 16. At the same time, the Union soldiers at Harper's Ferry were to move south to keep Confederate troops in the Valley in place. If the plan worked 35,000 Union troops would face only 22,000 Confederate ones. Knowing the Union plan, Beauregard called his troops in from the Valley, raising his forces to 32,000 men. Although the battle of Bull Run on July 21 was hard fought, Beauregard won. Had the South lost the battle the war would probably have ended quickly. Greenhow was complimented by Confederate president Jefferson Davis for her effective work.

Greenhow spent the summer of 1861 supplying information to the Confederacy. But she soon came under suspicion. Allan Pinkerton, the head of Union counterintelligence, began to keep an eye on her. There was a lot of traffic at her house, at all sorts of

Confederate General Pierre G.T. Beauregard who was aided by the spy Rose Greenhow.

hours, and she seemed to have a lot of boyfriends. On August 23 Pinkerton watched as a young army officer came along and knocked on her door. Greenhow opened it and right there on the front stoop he passed a large envelope to her. She hugged and kissed him. Pinkerton figured he had her redhanded and promptly arrested her. Rather than take her to a jail, he confined Greenhow to her house. This was a mistake. Pinkerton's agents were all men and they had to allow Greenhow privacy to change clothes and bathe. This gave her the chance to dispose of a lot of evidence. In addition, Pinkerton did not arrest her 12-year-old daughter, also named Rose. Little Rose was able to alert her mother's agents to keep away—soon she too was under house arrest.

Greenhow's confinement was not difficult. She charmed her jailer, army 1st Lieutenant N. E. Shelton, and he allowed her a lot of freedom. She could entertain guests and some of these were her agents. They carried information to Greenhow and she used them to pass information to Confederate forces in Virginia. One agent employed by the Senate Military Affairs Committee actually smuggled an important military map to her. Greenhow arranged to smuggle it out again, through the Union lines to the Confederacy! Early in 1862 Greenhow and her Little Rose were sent to the Old Capitol Prison. It was harder to run a spy ring from there, but Greenhow managed it. As a "lady," she was allowed visitors, who would bring her information. Sometimes she would pass information to her agents by fastening little notes to rubber balls that Little Rose would "accidentally" throw out a window. Messages were also concealed in "rats," little bunches of hair that were used in some of the fancier hairstyles of the day.

Meanwhile, Greenhow proved of great propaganda value to the Confederacy. After all, she was a refined lady who was being held in prison with her innocent little daughter. Finally, in June 1862 the Union decided to get rid of her and with Little Rose she was included in a prisoner exchange.

Greenhow was given a warm welcome in the South. She was a guest of President Davis and other prominent officials. However, after working as a spy for more than a year, she found life in Richmond pretty tame. In August 1863 Davis sent her to Europe to help drum up support for the Confederacy. She toured England and

France, where she was a guest of Emperor Napoleon III. While in Europe Greenhow wrote a book about her adventures which sold very well.

After a year in Europe, Greenhow decided to return to the Confederacy aboard the blockade runner *Condor*. Near Cape Fear, North Carolina, the ship was intercepted by a Union warship. While trying to escape, the *Condor* ran aground in rough seas. To avoid capture Greenhow tried to escape in a rowboat, but the boat capsized in heavy seas. Greenhow was carrying a lot of gold hidden in her clothing and the weight of the gold dragged her down and she drowned. Her body was later recovered and she was buried with full military honors.

The Mysterious Harrison. One of the most successful Confederate spies was a man named Harrison. But for more than 120 years no one knew much about him except his name. It seems that there were two Confederate spies named Harrison—James Harrison and Henry T. Harrison. But both were known in the records only as "Harrison." Both worked mostly in Virginia; both were eventually fired because they drank too much; and both men had acting experience—James was a professional and Henry an amateur. So it was not until the mid-1980s that historian James Hall managed to figure out which of the two was the important one, after carefully going through thousands of records at the National Archives.

Henry T. Harrison was born about 1832 in Mississippi. When the Civil War broke out he became a spy for Confederate forces in Virginia. Harrison was an excellent agent. His acting experience permitted him to maintain his cover for long periods. He was able to speak with many different accents and this was important because in those days people in many parts of the country spoke very differently. In the spring of

Confederate General James Longstreet was given much useful information by Harrison just before the battle of Gettysburg.

1863 Henry was assigned to Confederate Lieutenant General James Longstreet. Longstreet's forces were facing strong Union forces on the coast of Virginia. Longstreet sent Harrison to get information on Union forces around Norfolk and he did well, bringing a lot of useful information.

Longstreet's troops were soon transferred to the Confederate Army of Northern Virginia, under General Robert E. Lee. Lee's army was just below the Rappahannock River in central Virginia preparing to invade the North. This operation would lead to the great battle of Gettysburg. Just before the army marched, Longstreet gave Harrison a sack of gold coins. He told him to "bring back information of importance."

Sneaking through the Union lines, Harrison reached Washington, nearly 50 miles away. He disguised himself as a wealthy Unionist and in bars and restaurants Harrison treated Union officers to drinks. Some of them drank too much and talked too much. After about a week, Harrison decided he had enough information. He set out to find Longstreet. The general had not told him where the army was going. Harrison had to figure it out by reading Union newspapers. As he "followed" the Confederate forces, he encountered Union troops. He was able to take note of the location of most of the Union forces as he moved across Maryland and into Pennsylvania. Harrison reached the Confederates at Chambersburg, Pennsylvania, late on June 28, and was immediately arrested as a spy! The next morning Longstreet had him released— Harrison brought very important news.

Confederate forces had been operating with little useful information on Union movements. Harrison brought word that Major General George G. Meade had been placed in command of the Union Army of the Potomac. Meade was a much better general than the previous one. Harrison also had detailed information on the location of Union forces on the night of the 27th, just 36-hours earlier. The Union troops were only about 40 miles from Chambersburg. This was very important. General Lee, the Confederate commander, had believed that the Union army was still in Virginia. His army was scattered and with Union forces so close this was very dangerous. Harrison's information allowed Lee to concentrate his troops. Two days later a great battle began at Gettysburg that lasted for three days. The Confederates were defeated, but they were able to retreat to safety. Without the information brought by Harrison the scattered Confederate forces might have been destroyed.

Harrison was later fired because of drunkenness. In September Longstreet was ordered to take his troops to Georgia. Deciding he needed a good spy to accompany him, Longstreet tried to find Harrison but he had disappeared. Harrison had decided to go west and eventually settled in Montana. Harrison died in 1900. It would be 80 years before Henry T. Harrison was identified as the famous spy.

V

The Spy Catchers

*B*oth sides worked hard to detect and capture spies. Exactly how successful they were is hard to know. However the Union does seem to have been better at spy catching than the Confederacy. This is probably because the first Union spy catcher was Allan Pinkerton whom we have already met earlier in this book. Pinkerton was born in Scotland. His father was a policeman, but he became a cooper—a barrel maker. He came to America in 1842 and opened a cooperage in Illinois. A few years later he accidentally uncovered a ring of counterfeiters and was made a deputy sheriff. Then in 1847 Pinkerton sold his business and became a policeman in Chicago. In 1850 he was appointed the city's first detective. Soon afterwards he became a private detective in Chicago. He was the first private detective in America.

As you will remember, Pinkerton's connections with Lincoln and General McClellan caused him to be in charge of Union espionage and counterespionage. Although he wasn't a very good spy master,

Allan Pinkerton served the Union army as head of intelligence at the beginning of the war.

Pinkerton proved an excellent counterspy. After all, it was detective work, and he was very good at that. Pinkerton and his agents uncovered a plot to kill Lincoln as he journeyed to Washington to be sworn in as president. They also detected a conspiracy to stage an uprising in Maryland in the spring of 1861. Pinkerton's greatest success was in breaking Rose O'Neal Greenhow's spy ring in Washington. A lot of work went into breaking Greenhow's spy network. Pinkerton and his men kept her and her house under observation for a very long time, in all sorts of weather. But Pinkerton's failure as a spy master, and McClellan's removal from command, led to his being fired in late 1862. He returned to the private detective business, at which he was very successful. He died in 1884.

After Pinkerton's removal, Union counterespionage operations became the business of the provost marshal generals of the different armies. These were the chief military police officers of the army. After Pinkerton's break up of the Greenhow network, most Confederate spies operated on their own or with only a few henchmen. So none of the provost marshals gained much fame as spy catchers, although they were fairly successful at preventing serious losses of information to the Confederacy. Some of them were criticized because they seemed to be unable to stop smuggling between the North and the South but this was actually because they were busy managing the Union spy network. Many of the smugglers were actually spies and counterspies.

Confederate counterintelligence was very poor. Although some 60 people were executed in the South during the war, most of them do not seem to have been spies. Some of them were just Union sympathizers who were lynched by vigilantes. Early in the war the most important spy catcher of the Confederacy was Brigadier General John Henry Winder. He was born in 1800, and graduated from West Point in 1820, but by 1861 he was still only a major. He was a friend of Jefferson Davis, who had been one of his students at West Point in the late 1820s. When Davis became president of the Confederacy he made Winder the provost marshal of Richmond and central Virginia. This put Winder in charge of military police activities in the area, including counterespionage. But he wasn't

This sketch of the hanging of two Confederate spies appeared in the July 4, 1863, issue of Harper's Weekly.

very good at it. Like Pinkerton, he used civilian detectives to chase spies. Unlike Pinkerton, he had no experience in the detective business. His agents proved a clumsy lot. They bothered a lot of people but they never broke up the most important Union spy network in the South, Elizabeth Van Lew's ring. Winder wasn't a very suspicious man. Van Lew would even sometimes drop in on him for a chat and Winder granted her permission to visit Union prisoners held in Richmond. He often gave her passes to travel outside of Richmond. She used these passes to send messages to Union generals. Winder was later transferred from the job of provost marshal and put in charge of supplying prisoners-of-war. He wasn't very good at this job either, although he tried very hard. He died from exhaustion and overwork just before the end of the war, in early 1865. There were no other important Confederate spy catchers.

VI

Codes and Ciphers
of the Civil War

*T*o keep information secret it is often concealed by various methods of "secret writing." These are commonly called "codes." This is actually incorrect. A code is a special type of secret writing.

A code uses a system of random letters or numbers to represent words. Coded information looks like gibberish. For example, *xhxe gjop tnbw retw* might stand for "General Grant arrives tomorrow." Codes require special dictionaries called "code books." These contain endless lists of words, each of which has its own distinct group of letters or numbers. There is no connection between the code group and the actual word. While *gprc* might stand for "cattle," "battle" might be *qopn*, and "bottle" *fjki*. Codes are very difficult to break because nothing actually means anything. They are also difficult to construct, and require a lot of work to use. As a result genuine codes were not used much during the Civil War. But improvised codes were sometimes used. One simple system was what might be called the "identical dictionary" code. An agent

used exactly the same dictionary his handler had. Words were assigned numbers according to their order in the dictionary; for example, 13414 might mean the 14th word on page 134. This was clumsy, but useful for simple messages. There was also some use of code phrases. A code phrase is merely a sentence that may make perfect sense, but actually means something entirely different. For example, "I enjoyed reading *The Three Musketeers*" might really mean "Send reinforcements quick." Of course you can't send long messages using code phrases.

The most common form of secret writing used during the Civil War was the cipher. A cipher is a system of scrambling the contents of a message to conceal its meaning. Ciphers are not as difficult to break as genuine codes. This is because a cipher is really just based on scrambling the alphabet. It may only take a handful of messages to enable a skilled cryptographer to break a cipher—only a few words have two letters, only a few more have three, and some letters occur in patterns, such as "th," "tt," or "qu." Ciphers were well-known among many people in America in the years before the Civil War because Edgar Allen Poe had used a cipher in his famous mystery story *The Gold Bug.*

The basis of any cipher is very simple. Take, for example, the one used by Elizabeth Van Lew. It was found written on a tiny piece of paper hidden in the back of her watch after she died.

Elizabeth Van Lew's Cipher Grid

1st Digit ---->	6	R	N	B	H	T	X
(Row Number)	3	V	1	U	8	4	W
	1	E	M	3	J	5	G
	5	L	A	9	0	I	D
	2	K	7	2	Z	6	S
	4	P	O	Y	C	F	Q
2nd Digit----->		1	3	6	2	5	4
(Column Number)							

Notice that rows and columns are numbered randomly. To encipher a letter or number you use the digits of its row and column.

Try enciphering the phrase "Send 12 horses." The letter "s" is in row 2, column 4, and is written as 24. The "e" is in row 1, column 1, or 11. The "n" is 63. And so on. Enciphered, the phrase reads 24116354 3326 624361242324. To make it difficult for anyone to break the cipher you can chop the message up into groups of four or five letters. Since the numbers don't always divide neatly by four or five, you have to add a few additional ones—called nulls—to make everything come out even. Broken into groups of five and with some nulls added, the phrase now reads 24116 35433 26624 36124 23243 26479. The last six digits, "3 26479" are the nulls, and have no meaning.

Van Lew's cipher had several flaws. First, you needed a copy of the grid to use it. Worse, she seems to have used the same cipher for all her messages. She was very lucky that none of her messages were ever inter-

Virgenere Table

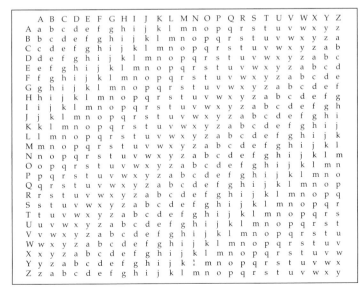

cepted. Had that happened it would not have taken long for a clever cryptographer to break the cipher. Any cipher can be broken. All you need is samples of the cipher in use and some time.

The principal Confederate cipher was based on what is known as a Virgenere Table, named after a Frenchman who invented it in the 1700s.

A Virgenere Table uses a key phrase to generate a cipher. To encipher a message you find the plain text letter on the left side of the table, and check it against the key phrase letter across the top. Using the key phrase *Come retribution*, we can encipher the message "Enemy forces are retreating."

Plain Text Message:	E n e m y f o r c e s a r e re t r e a ti n g
Key Phrase:	c o m e r e t r i b u t i o n c o m e re t r i
Ciphered Message:	g a q q p j h i k f n t z s e g h d i t x b e o

In this message checking the first "e" in plain text under the c-column gives us a "g." The plain text "n," checked in the o-column, is an "a." The second "e," gives a "q" in the m-column. And so forth. So "enemy forces are retreating" becomes *gaqqp jhikfn tzs eghditxbeo*, which we can scramble further by breaking up into groups of four or five letters and adding nulls.

Using the table took time and it was easy to make mistakes. To replace the table someone invented a cipher wheel. It was made of two disks of wood, on which the letters of the alphabet were carved. By rotating the disks, using the key phrase as a guide, the wheel produced exactly the same ciphers as the table in much less time.

The Confederates made a big mistake in their use of this cipher. They failed to change their key phrases often enough. In fact, they only used three throughout the entire war; *Manchester Bluff, Complete Victory,* and, right near the end, for only a few messages, *Come Retribution.* Any cipher can be broken if there are enough examples of it available.

The Confederacy's Virgenere cipher was broken by three young Union cipher experts. David Homer Bates, Albert Chandler, and Charles Tinker hadn't set out to become cipher experts. When the Civil War began they were teenage telegraph operators. Andrew Carnegie, who was later a famous millionaire and philanthropist, helped set up the United States Military Telegraph Corps. He hired the three young men. The main office of the USMTC was at the War Department, a few steps from the White House. There messages would come and go at all hours. President Lincoln often visited and sat with the operators. Since the office was the most secret place in Washington, it was one of the few places the president could be alone. It was so private he often went there when he had problems to think about. It was in the telegraph office that Lincoln wrote the Emancipation Proclamation.

Telegraph messages had to be enciphered, in case they were intercepted by the Confederates. So the telegraph operators soon became experts at enciphering and deciphering Union messages. These messages were sent in various ciphers, some of which used a wheel similar to the Confederate one. Union scouts and spies often intercepted Confederate messages. Although they were in cipher, they were passed on to the USMTC in Washington. Soon the young men began working on the Confederate cipher. After a lot of hard work they broke the cipher, because most of the messages were based on the key phrase *Complete Victory.* Nicknamed the "Sacred Three," by the end of the war Bates, Chandler, and Tinker were routinely deciphering all Confederate messages that came their way. The information they supplied was enormously useful to the Union.

Yet another method of sending a message was the "route cipher." A "route cipher" scrambled the order of the words in a message. The words would then also be enciphered using a normal cipher. The example below is a very simple example, written by President Lincoln. Can you read it?

1	2	3	4	5	6	7
Washington, D.C.	July	15th	18	60	3	for
Sigh	man	Cammer	on	period	I	would
give	much	to be	relieved	of the	impression	that
Meade	comma	Couch	comma	Smith	and	all
comma	since	the	battle	of	get	ties
burg	comma	have	striven	only	to	get
the enemy	over	the river	wihtout	another	fight	period
please	tell	me	if	you	know	who
was	the	one	corps	commander	who	was
for	fighting	comma	in the	council	of	war
on	Sunday	night	signature	A. Lincoln	Bless	him

The first line seems pretty easy, "Washington, D.C., July 15th, 1863." But then it gets confusing. The next few words, from "for" to "period" are "padding," nonsense added to the message to make it more difficult to read. The message actually begins with the "I" in the second line. The words after "A. Lincoln" are also padding, though they perhaps also express the cipher clerk's devotion to the president. Notice the odd way of spelling "Gettysburg" and that periods and commas have been written out. Some route ciphers actually had lines that had to be read backwards, or from the top down, or in other strange ways. Often code words would be substituted for actual words or phrases, such as "oyster" for "battle" and "Nuts" for "Abraham Lincoln," to further confuse decryption. Then the message would be sent by columns, with all the words in column 1 being sent before those in column 2, and so forth. Although the

Union sent about 6.5 million messages using several dozen different route ciphers, the Confederates never broke a single one.

Aside from codes and ciphers, there were other ways of sending secret messages. A black couple named Dabney who served as spies for the Union army in the spring of 1863 had one. Mr. Dabney was with the Union army north of the Rappahannock River in Virginia. Mrs. Dabney worked as a cook and laundress at the headquarters of a Confederate general south of the river. She was in a good position to over-hear important information. Mrs. Dabney would communicate with Mr. Dabney using a clothesline. As Mr. Dabney explained:

That there gray shirt is Longstreet; and when she takes it off, it means he's gone down about Richmond. That white shirt means Hill, and when she moves it up to the west end of the line Hill has moved upstream. That red one is Stonewall [Jackson]. He's down on the right now, and if he moves, she will move that red shirt.

Union Secret Service men meeting during the Peninsular campaign, May 1862.

AFTERWORD

A Lost Story

When the Civil War ended the Union had one of the best intelligence systems in the world. It had a wide reach. Union agents operated in Europe, Cuba, Puerto Rico, and the West Indies. They kept an eye on people raising money and supplies for the South. There were Union agents in Mexico, which French Emperor Napoleon III was trying to take over. Union cryptographic skills were among the best in the world. But even as the Union army—a million strong—was quickly disbanded, so too was the Union's intelligence service. Soon America again no longer had an intelligence service. And once again, as in the years before the Civil War, if the president needed some vital information he had to improvise by sending a friend or a military officer on a secret mission. Not until the 1880s did the United States begin to set up a formal military intelligence system, when the navy opened a small office to collect information. Thereafter a real intelligence system gradually developed, although it took

until after World War II, over 80 years *after* the Civil War, for a modern system to be created.

Meanwhile, even the history of intelligence operations during the Civil War was lost. Many of the records were destroyed. Other records were put in storage and forgotten. There was a small flood of memoirs by people who had been spies, or who claimed to have been spies. But most of these books, such as those by Belle Boyd or Allan Pinkerton, were so full of errors they were often of little value, and some actually were completely ficticious, but almost everything written about espionage during the Civil War came to be based on these memoirs. Not until the mid-1990s were some of the original records discovered, quite by accident. So only now is a more accurate picture of espionage during the Civil War coming to light. It is a story that has waited nearly 150 years to be told.

Glossary

abolitionist	A person who worked for the abolishment of slavery.
break	To find the solution to a code or cipher; also "crack."
code	A letter or number system in which each set or group of letters or numbers represents a particular word. Coded messages may also be enciphered.
Confederacy	The Southern states that seceded from the Union formed a new country called the Confederate States of America—the Confederacy.
Confederate	A citizen of the Confederate States of America.
counterespionage or counterintelligence	The business of catching spies.
counterspy	A person engaged in the business of counterintelligence—catching spies.
cryptographer	Someone who works at inventing and breaking codes and ciphers.
cipher	The use of simple letter or number substitution to conceal the meaning of a message. Often wrongly called a "code." Sometimes written "cypher" during the Civil War.
decipher	To take a ciphered message and translate it into "plain text."
decode	To take a coded message and translate it into "plain text."
double agent	Someone working as an agent for one side, while pretending to be an agent of the other.
encode	To translate something into a code.

encipher	To translate something so that its meaning is scrambled using a cipher.
master spy	Someone who is a particularly effective spy.
nulls	Meaningless groups of letters or words added to ciphered or coded messages to make them more difficult to break.
Secret Service	In the Civil War this described anyone assigned to operations of a secret nature, including not only spies but people secretly sent to purchase weapons or raise money, and so forth. The real Secret Service had actually been formed within the Treasury Department in 1860, for the purpose of catching counterfeiters. Some Secret Service agents served as spies and intelligence gatherers during the Civil War.
secessionist	Southerners who voted to secede from the Union and form a new republic.
spy	Someone who secretly seeks information about the enemy's activities.
spy master	The person responsible for supervising spies.

Further Reading

Because they are based on memoirs, most books about espionage during the Civil War are not very good. After all, the former spies who wrote about themselves were inclined to inflate their achievements. And some of the memoirs are outright fabrications, really works of fiction by people who had little or no connection with intelligence operations during the war.

The best single book about espionage during the Civil War is Edwin C. Fishel's *The Secret War for the Union: The Untold Story of Military Intelligence in the Civil War* (Boston: Houghton Mifflin, 1996). It is the only serious book on the subject. Based on surviving official documents, letters, and diaries, as well as the memoirs of some of the people involved, it is a very large volume. It is 700 pages long and not suitable for younger readers.

There are, however, some other books that are of use to younger readers:

Some Reliable Books about Espionage in the Civil War

Markle, Donald. *Spies and Spymasters of the Civil War.* New York: Hippocrene, 1994.

Martin, Jane A. and Ross, Jeremy (editors). *Spies, Scouts, and Raiders.* Alexandria, Va.: Time-Life Books, 1985.

Reit, Seymour. *Behind Rebel Lines: The Incredible Story of Emma Edmonds, Civil War Spy.* New York: Harcourt Brace, 1991.

Some Reliable Memoirs about Espionage in the Civil War

Bates, David Homer. *Lincoln in the Telegraph Office: Recollections of the United States Military Telegraph Corps during the Civil War.*

Edmonds, Sarah Emma. *Nurse and Spy in the Union Army.*

Sorrel, Moxey G. *Recollections of a Confederate Staff Officer.*

Some Unreliable Memoirs about Espionage in the Civil War (which can be a lot of fun to read)

Boyd, Belle. *Belle Boyd in Camp and Prison.* Extremely unreliable, but often very exciting tales by the South's self-proclaimed "greatest female spy."

Van Doren Stern, Philip. *Secret Missions of the Civil War.* Selections from the memoirs of many Civil War spies and purported spies from both sides.

Velazquez, Loreta Janeta. *The Woman in Battle: A Narrative of Exploits, Adventures, and Travels of Madam.* Possibly the most unreliable book ever written about the Civil War—but very entertaining.

Websites About Spies in the Civil War

Bowser, Mary Elizabeth:
http://www.brightmoments.com/blackhistory/nmeb.html

Confederate Cipher Wheel:
http://members.aol.com/ubchi2/cipher.htm

Greenhow, Rose O'Neal:
http://scriptorium.lib.duke.edu/greenhow/

Rochester 9th Grader Pages:
http://www.rochester.k12.mn.us/john-marshall/overton/cwproj/topics/spies.html

Index

PHOTO CREDITS
Franklin D. Roosevelt Library: p. 23; *Harper's Weekly* : pp. 14, 16 (bottom), 42, 48; Library of
Congress: pp. 10, 16 (top), 17, 18, 19, 34, 35, 37, 46, 56; Lincoln Museum: pp. 22; National Archives:
pp.30, 39; United States Army Military History Institute: p. 25